Intersections Between Music and Mental Health:

Exploring Music and Psychological Functioning

Written by Brenden Hiebert and Austin Mardon

Intersections Between Music and Mental Health:

Exploring Music and Psychological Functioning

Written by Brenden Hiebert and Austin Mardon
Edited by Jessica Jutras and Catherine Mardon
Designed by Clare Dalton and Typestting by Dana Mah

GM
PRESS

Cover Design by Clare Dalton ,Typesetting by Dana Mah

Print ISBN 978-1-77369-820-5
E-book ISBN 978-1-77369-821-2

Golden Meteorite Press
103 11919 82 St NW
Edmonton, AB T5B 2W3
www.goldenmeteoritepress.com

Dedication

To my sister Jaclyn

All our dreams can come true,
if we have the courage to pursue them

-Walt Disney

Aknowledgements

I would like to thank Austin Mardon, Jessica Jutras, and the rest of the AIC team for the opportunity and their endless support in making this book a reality.

Table of Contents

Introduction

In Canada, "By age 40, about 50% of the population will have or have had a mental illness" (Mental Health Commission of Canada, 2013). This staggering statistic reveals that mental illness affects "people of all ages, education, income levels, and cultures" and the effects of this have the potential to ripple throughout various aspects of a person's life. Strained relationships with oneself and others can further affect a person's self image and worth regardless of what stage of life they are at. Seemingly simple or familiar tasks can start to feel burdensome and one's ability to work and maintain a healthy life can be seriously impacted. In recent years, progress has been made to de-stigmatize mental illness and mental health related concerns, especially around the causation and treatment of such. Our current understanding presents that "A complex interplay of genetic, biological, personality, and environmental factors cause mental [illness]," however, suicide remains as a leading cause of death in all person's from adolescence all the way through middle age. This alone is evidence of the continued work that needs to be done and how crucial recognizing and treating mental illness is. Thus, this text aims to engage with the topics in a way that is both informative and empathetic in order to appropriately engage in the discussion and simultaneously contribute to the dissolution of stigma around mental illness.

Introduction Reference:
Canadian Mental Health Association. (2013, July 19). Fast Facts about Mental Illness. CMHA
National. https://cmha.ca/fast-facts-about-mental-illness

Chapter 1: Anxiety Disorders

"In 2013, an estimated 3 million Canadians (11.6%) aged 18 years or older reported that they had a mood and/or anxiety disorder" (Public Health Agency of Canada, 2015). While this statistic reflects the adult population, it is entirely possible for these disorders to emerge at any stage of life. This is because genetics, stress, life altering events, or a combination of such can serve as a trigger. An additional factor that may contribute to the prevalence of anxiety and mood disorders is the nature in which they become intertwined or directly caused by the presence of other conditions. They also frequently coexist in a dynamic relationship where the existence of one may be the dominant cause for the other. This isn't exclusive to just mood and anxiety disorders either. For example, schizoaffective disorder is the combination between schizophrenic symptoms and mood disorder symptoms. Fortunately, this overlap applies to treatment options and outcomes where improvement in one often translates to improvement in the other, i.e., generalized anxiety caused by manic depression tends to lessen as the manic depression is treated. Unfortunately, the opposite can also be true, where the worsening of one condition may increase the severity of the other, potentially resulting in a feedback loop. Despite this relationship, however, mood disorders will be addressed in the next chapter.

While feeling nervous or anxious at certain points in life is normal and part of being human, people with anxiety experience intense feelings of fear analogous to a fight or flight response that may be deemed extreme considering the circumstance or trigger. Symptoms of anxiety range from general feelings of worry and muscle tension in a mild response to trembling, dizziness, and an increased heart rate in a more severe response. The exact symptoms that someone might exhibit often depends on the individual and the type of anxiety they experience. For example, somebody with a mild phobia may feel tense or upset around the trigger but display fewer external symptoms than somebody with more severe anxiety experiencing a panic attack. According to Statistics Canada (2012), there are various anxiety disorders, such as, generalized anxiety disorder (GAD), panic disorder, post traumatic stress disorder, and obsessive-compulsive disorder (OCD). Phobias such as agoraphobia and social phobia also fall under this category. This chapter will focus mostly on GAD and OCD, with the former being the most common form of anxiety and classified as "Generalized and persistent excessive anxiety and worry that is accompanied by somatic symptoms" (Statistics Canada, 2012). While most findings and practises will generalize across the various anxiety disorders, it's important to note that each individual, source, and response is unique and should be treated as such.

For individuals living with GAD, "The exact cause … is unknown but there are likely a number of factors that contribute to the disorder" (Statistics Canada, 2012). As mentioned previously, the source of a person's GAD is complicated and often speculation. Regardless, "Everyday concerns such as work, health or finances can cause marked discomfort and distress" (Statistics Canada, 2012). This can lead to a higher baseline of stress during the day that can feel unrelenting when daily experiences act as triggers. One consequence of this is an increase in feelings of exhaustion and lethargy during down time away from these triggers should the GAD be ignored. Fortunately, "Individuals with GAD frequently seek treatment. The two most common treatments are medication and psychotherapy, which can be taken alone or in combination" (Statistics Canada, 2012). Medication and therapy are universal in the realm of managing mental illness and are the most common forms of treatment outside of an individual's own methods of self-care and mediation. In terms of anxiety medications, "Benzodiazepines … are effective for symptom reduction but are highly addictive and therefore can only be taken for short periods of time" (Statistics Canada, 2012). Examples of these medications include Valium, Xanax, and Ativan, all of which are strong tranquilizers that are effective at treating severe anxiety responses but can be dangerous if used long term or in combination with alcohol or other drugs. An option with less potential side effects is, "Buspirone, another anti anxiety medication, [that] is also effective and can be used on an ongoing basis" (Statistics Canada, 2012). This drug isn't chemically related to benzodiazepines and doesn't produce strong sedation effects in the user but still shouldn't be mixed with alcohol. Finally, a common therapy for anxiety is cognitive behavioural therapy. While there are a variety of techniques with CBT, the common aim is to "help the individual … identify negative thoughts and behaviours and replace them with positive ones" (Statistics Canada, 2012).

One way that music can benefit those with anxiety is with managing somatic or physical symptoms. Similar to how breathing techniques can be used to slow down an increased heart rate or racing thoughts, music can achieve a similar result through sympathetically attending to our emotional needs. Every person has their own taste in music and range of needs and so there is a wide variety of effective music choices across different people. What works for one person may not be as effective for others. However, outside of these tastes, there are certain aspects and kinds of music that could be generally categorized as relaxing, soft, or otherwise soothing.

One way to begin analyzing why certain kinds of music may be rewarding and ultimately useful for mood regulation is to understand some of the ways that we distinguish between different instruments and ultimately perceive music. The timbre of an instrument refers to the quality of its sound in regards to its harmonic content. For example, this is how you can tell the difference between a flute and a guitar even when they play the same note. The arrangement of overtones or integers of the fundamental frequency make up all the complexities of sound, which is why this concept is so important to music as a whole. Distortion pedals for electric guitars are essentially adding harmonics to enrich the sound and this added complexity makes consonant intervals like the perfect fifth and octave sound full, hence the popularity of the power chord, yet more dissonant intervals or denser chords get unintelligible. Interestingly, the majority of the harmonic information and our perception of timbre happens in the transient or attack of the note. The transient only lasts for the first few milliseconds of a disturbance such as a string being plucked, and without hearing that, we can be fooled into thinking it was from an entirely different instrument. Now if we consider a full orchestra, each section produces a unique series of overtones that interact to create a harmonically rich experience. Furthermore, within each section, each instrument plays with slight differences in pitch and tone that sum together to create the full sound orchestras are known for.

In music therapy and research, classical music is often a source of interest, likely due to the cultural shift following the emergence of the Mozart effect that claimed listening to Mozart's music and other classical pieces may temporarily increase intelligence, specifically in children. Regardless of the accuracy to that claim, classical music's ability to affect mood, productivity, and behaviour is constantly being explored. While the form of classical music does vary piece to piece and across different eras, there is consistently a strong sense of order and structure not unlike the way we tell stories, even today. For example, in literature, motifs are repeated symbols or phrases that recur throughout a story. Similarly, in music, motifs are repeated ideas that recur throughout a song or larger collection of music. While motifs are present in film scores to pop music, in classical works, the focus of the piece is usually on those motifs and the way they develop and evolve as the song progresses. Alongside the similarities to storytelling, the absence of lyrics acts as an opportunity for us to create or find meaning in the melody and arrangement. In this way, classical music may act as an escape to a world within the music and allow listeners to find peace in where it takes them.

Instrumental music is frequently used to mitigate nerves and promote relaxation in situations from the massage parlour to the operating room. Stripped down or acoustic versions of songs can be effective in this setting because of the lower levels of energy that come from sparse arrangements and often slower tempos than the original. Mirroring this can help calm us down, however, favourite or familiar music is also effective even if it's high in energy and complexity because of the emotional value it holds. What's really important is creating an appropriate atmosphere that minimizes stress and worry to ultimately facilitate the reduction of physical symptoms.

In a recent study in India, the researchers found that, "Around 50% [of] children exposed to music therapy experienced no preoperative anxiety at posttest" (S.K. et al., 2020, p. 648). Their experimental group experienced approximately 76.1% reduction in anxiety levels following the music therapy. In determining these results, they used a 3 arm randomized control trial to assess the effectiveness of music therapy as well as visual imagery techniques on 36 children aged between 4 to 12 years old who were dealing with preoperative anxiety. While the study consisted of a small sample size, the results appear quite remarkable considering how frequent and challenging anxiety can be to a child and their family during the preoperative period. Anxiety can actually have serious implications on the procedure since sleep patterns, cooperativeness, and response to anesthesia can all be affected resulting in complications and increased cost. The data was gathered using the Hamilton Anxiety rating scale where multiple questions are asked and rated by the patient on a scale of 0-4 with the combined points equating to their approximate level of anxiety. The results of the study suggest that "Certain interventions like music may provide a viable alternative to sedatives and anti-anxiety drugs for reducing preoperative anxiety" (S.K. et al., 2020, p. 645). Being able to avoid medications that have serious side effects such as benzodiazepines in children and others is an important goal and hopefully more studies will work to replicate these findings.

Statistics Canada (2012) presents obsessive-compulsive disorder, or OCD, as a disorder that is characterized by obsessions, compulsions, or both. These obsessions are persistent, unwanted thoughts that produce intense anxiety that is then eased by performing repetitive and ritual-like compulsions. This can create a cycle that's difficult to break since the compulsion negatively reinforces the obsession by taking away or reducing the anxiety. Similar to generalized anxiety disorder, there isn't one definitive cause of OCD. However, unlike GAD, fewer people seek immediate treatment with roughly a "10-year gap between the onset of symptoms and seeking help, with the receipt of a correct diagnosis and/or treatment potentially taking another 7 years." Part of the reason for this may be that those struggling with OCD know their obsessions and compulsions can be irrational and their natural urge to resist them can lead to them also resisting treatment. In terms of treatment, "Serotonin reuptake inhibitors (antidepressants) are often prescribed and are effective in reducing the obsessive-compulsive symptoms. Behavioural therapy may also be prescribed so that individuals with OCD can face the situations that cause them anxiety and attempt to de-sensitize them" (Statistics Canada, 2012). Compared to GAD, OCD treatment and diagnosis appears more complicated with not as many people seeking treatment or receiving the correct diagnosis. If left untreated, OCD can be debilitating both mentally and physically and impair someone's ability to function on a day to day basis.

Social events, public speaking, and performing music can all be anxiety inducing for many people. In the case of music performance, the very act can have a lot of personal and emotional attachments regarding our abilities and feelings, especially when it's original music. This performance anxiety could then be described as the "Experience of persisting, distressful apprehension about and/or actual impairment of, performance skills in a public context, to a degree unwarranted given the individual's aptitude, training, and level of preparation" (Salmon, 1990, as cited in McGrath, 2017, p. 11). The exact cause can range but the fear of being judged and the fear of failure frequently provoke symptoms, and "[a]s you anticipate technical failure or a subpar performance, your body may react as if it had actually happened" (McGrath, 2017, p. 12). This suggests that the worry and mentality around making a mistake will make someone more likely to actually mess up than if they weren't attending to those thoughts. Many musicians and bands have their own rituals before performing that can help with nerves similar to how an athlete or team would prepare before a game. While the effects of these are placebo, they can still be effective to the extent that they diminish pre-emptive mental and physical symptoms of anxiety. Unfortunately, this uncomfortable side of performing is often less talked about. Some musicians still feel anxious but have mastered hiding it, and some may simply convince themselves that symptoms like nausea and light-headedness are normal or an unavoidable part of performing. This shouldn't have to be the case and fortunately now more than ever there is treatment available to help reframe fearful emotions and anxious symptoms into feelings of excitement and anticipation.

"Championed in the 1960s by Nobel Prize laureate for medicine Sir James Black, beta-blockers have been used extensively to offset the physical symptoms of stage fright, such as heart palpitations, hyperventilation, hand tremor, and nausea" (Hingley, 1985, as cited in McGrath, 2017, p. 69). Beta-blockers work by blocking adrenaline, which causes an increase in heart rate and blood pressure. While there is notable evidence of this medication mediating the symptoms of performance anxiety, it's important to note that it doesn't actually get to the root cause of those symptoms. The medications then are really treating the symptoms of the anxiety but not the anxiety itself. This is where therapy and counseling may be a more effective and long term solution for certain anxieties. Exposure therapy, for example, is common in treating fears and phobias with the focus being on presenting the stimulus like a performance in the absence of a reinforcer like making a mistake and getting booed off stage. The advantage of doing so can help the person rationalize the phobia and confront their fear. Avoidance behaviour on the other hand will usually achieve the opposite result by reinforcing that it is something to fear. It also introduces other negative emotions like guilt and doubt towards that activity that contribute to the anxiety. But for exposure therapy, it is important to move incrementally and not all at once. For example, spending time practising and playing on a stage without an audience may be the first step in overcoming the fear. Then, a series of smaller performances and stage experiences that build up in magnitude could lead to the reduction or elimination of the fear. Progressing slowly is important since further negative performance experiences are likely to have an adverse effect. Overall, identifying and addressing the root cause of one's anxiety head on is the best path towards the healthy management of symptoms.

Chapter 1 References:

McGrath C., Hendricks K.S., & Smith T.D. (2017). Performance Anxiety Strategies: A

Musician's Guide to Managing Stage Fright. Rowman & Littlefield Publishers.

Public Health Agency of Canada. (2015, June 3). Mood and anxiety disorders in Canada -

Canada.ca. Retrieved from the Government of Canada Website: https://www.canada.

ca/en/public-health/services/publications/diseases-conditions/mood-anxiety-disorders-canada.html

S.K., M., A., P., Rathord, K., & Kothari, S. (2020, June). Effectiveness of Music Therapy and

Visual Imagery Techniques on Preoperative Anxiety among Children Undergoing

Surgeries in Selected Hospitals of RajasthanPilot Study. Indian Journal of Public Health

Research & Development, 11(6), 644-649.

Statistics Canada. (2012, January 30). Section B - Anxiety disorders. Retrieved from the Statistics

Canada website: https://www150.statcan.gc.ca/n1/pub/82-619-m/2012004/sections/secti

onb-eng.htm#archived

Chapter 2: Mood Disorders

"Mood disorders are a group of mental illnesses that affect how you feel and think about yourself, other people and life in general" (Canadian Mental Health Association, 2013). Some predominant symptoms of mood disorders include the loss of motivation for previously interesting tasks, lethargy, feelings of guilt and worthlessness, and greater fluctuations in mood. Symptoms may vary depending on the mood disorder and other interpersonal differences, like how it's possible to "Experience psychosis during an episode of severe depression or mania" (Canadian Mental Health Association, 2013). The cause of these disorders can vary wildly from genetics, significant life stressors, and relationships, to childbirth, seasonal changes, and substance abuse. However, there is no one definitive cause for mood disorders and it is likely that a combination of factors contribute to their development. In this chapter we will discuss three of the main mood disorders: depression, dysthymia, and bipolar disorder. "Globally, more than 264 million people of all ages suffer from depression" (WHO, 2020). As one of the most common mental illnesses, "Depression is a leading cause of disability worldwide and is a major contributor to the overall global burden of disease" (WHO, 2020). Depressive episodes can last from two weeks to several months or longer if left untreated, and can severely impair one's ability to function and enjoy life. On top of the mental battle, those with depression may experience negative changes to their sleeping patterns, memory, and immune system among other changes. There are various medications aimed to help with depression such as, selective serotonin reuptake inhibitors (SSRIs), serotonin and norepinephrine reuptake inhibitors (SNRIs), or dopamine reuptake blockers. Most of these medications target the chemical balance in the brain, and in those previously mentioned, prevent the reuptake of neurotransmitters like serotonin, norepinephrine, and dopamine, increasing their availability. Antidepressants may also be combined with other medications like antipsychotics or pain medications to increase effectiveness. Unfortunately, many medications do have side effects that may make some symptoms worse such as insomnia, fatigue, or a general worsening of the condition. It is also common to experience withdrawal symptoms when quitting antidepressants if done so abruptly. Even with treatment, "Depression is a highly recurrent disorder with significant personal and public health consequences" (Burcusa, 2007, p. 959). This means that individuals who have previously had depression may be more at risk of having it in the future, especially for those with long-term cases.

2020 was a year synonymous with the COVID-19 virus. With stay at home orders, unemployment, and isolation, cases of mental health concern rose drastically. "During the pandemic, about 4 in 10 adults in the U.S. have reported symptoms of anxiety or depressive disorder, a share that has been largely consistent, up from one in ten adults who reported these symptoms from January to June 2019" (Panchal et al., 2021). In a meta-analysis involving COVID-19 patients, they noted that "Isolated people often have psychological stress reactions to various factors" (Chen et al., 2021, p. 1). This is supported by the increase in symptoms of mood and anxiety disorders during this time. Furthermore, "Confirmed patients accepted isolation treatment and other prevention and control measures, which leads to anxiety, stress, loneliness, depression, and despair" (Zhong et al., 2021, as cited in Chen et al., 2021, p. 2). For most patients there wasn't much of a choice, especially when refusing to isolate might have meant putting loved ones in danger. One of the hardest hit demographics was the elderly who had many procedures delayed by months and were unable to see visitors or spouses on top of being more susceptible to the disease. Lastly, it was observed that "Excessively negative emotions can result in obsessive thinking, and, in severe cases, psychopathy seriously affects the treatment and recovery of COVID-19 patients" (Chen et al., 2021, p. 2). Dysthymia or persistent depressive disorder is a condition very similar to depression. It is a mood disorder with similar causation and symptoms however it varies in the way it persists in an individual. For somebody with depression, they may experience a few weeks of symptoms followed by a period of relief or wellness. In people with dysthymia, the symptoms stay consistent, but often less severe. However, it is common for there to still be waves of depressive episodes that, when combined with dysthymia, can lead to more severe symptoms. Many of the same medications for depression are applicable to dysthymia, as well as other therapy methods. One of the biggest changes often comes from the lifestyle changes by the patient themselves. Exercise, improved sleep habits, and a balanced diet are often at the forefront of self maintenance, especially when it comes to mental health. However, these changes on their own may not be enough. Therapy with a professional can be an effective method to better understand the individual causes behind an individual's suffering. Interventions such as cognitive behavioural therapy (CBT) aim to identify problematic ways of thinking as well as empower individuals with the tools to deal with the triggers that have given the person trouble in the past.

Listening to music during difficult times is a common self coping mechanism. However, the kind of music different people gravitate towards in a crisis can differ to a significant degree depending on the person and the situation they're going through. Even simplifying the discussion to happy versus sad music doesn't necessarily narrow down the search as much as it would first seem.

The trouble begins with identifying what exactly constitutes happy and sad music. From a music theory perspective, most people are taught early on that major chords and keys are happy and minor chords and keys are sad. While this simplification helps with basic ear training, harmony, songwriting, and the contextual analysis of music can get far more complex. In western popular music, the octave is divided equally into twelve tones tuned relative to standard pitch (A=440 Hz) in what's called equal temperament. These twelve tones are the starting place for the 12 major/minor keys that tell you which 7 unique tones of the 12 are considered inside the key. The collection of notes changes depending on the key but the scale order or distance between the notes is the same across all 12 keys. This order, also known as the major scale, is best explained in whole tones and semitones. A semitone is the smallest step in this musical system and is the distance from one of the twelve tones to the one directly next to it. A whole tone, on the other hand, is made up of two semitones, so it skips over a step on our 12 tone ladder. A major scale is then made up of 2 whole tones, a semitone, 3 more whole tone leaps, and another semitone to return to the start of the scale. From this scale, the most common chords are made in stacks of thirds that create the harmony that our songs come from.

Now for minor scales, the relative minor scale shares the same collection of tones as its major counterpart, but the order of these notes begins in a different place. This is because the first chord of this minor scale is actually the sixth chord of the major scale. So the order for a natural minor scale would be a whole tone, a semitone, 2 whole tones, a semitone, and 2 more whole tones. Parallel minor scales begin on the same note as their major counterpart but have the same order as the relative minor scale and thus a different collection of notes. While there are many more scales and substitute chords like the sixth and seventh degree of minor scales frequently being raised by a semitone for more harmonic options, the main difference is that major keys resolve to a home chord that is major and minor keys resolve to a home chord that is minor. The interesting part is that musicians borrow from and modulate across these major and minor keys all the time. Furthermore, major keys have minor chords in their progression, but don't feel sad in context. The opposite is true for minor keys. This breaks the mold of happy and sad tonalities into more complex options that allow for deeper harmony and emotional expression. In fact, the range of emotions we experience from music is never black and white but a unique array of colours. What really defines the meaning of a chord is the context behind it, combined with other musical elements like timbre, arrangement, and the melodic phrasing.

The second half of this discussion relates to the lyrical content of music. Aside from the musical aspects previously discussed, we are tuned into the way a vocalist performs and even more so to the words being sung. A harmonically happy sounding song with devastatingly sad lyrics will drastically complicate our perception of this song. This is because the impact of the words outweighs what is being implied by the music, oftentimes creating more complicated and emotionally impactful work. Understating difficult things or framing them in an unexpected manner can be more powerful than portraying them at face value. The same can be said when a song that implies sadness through its music cues comes with lyrics that speak of love or otherwise. It can be empowering and emotionally charged because there's additional conflict within the music.

When it comes to choosing a song during a difficult time, we often search for songs that mirror our situations or emotions back to us. In this way, sad music could be seen as a way to dig deeper into our feelings. It can also be cathartic to know that other people have lived through similar experiences. Sad songs may also suggest that a person is more open to addressing their problems and more in touch with their emotions than somebody who only listens to happy music. However, it can sometimes promote extended periods of antisocial behaviour during difficult times. On the other hand, happy songs can be effective at helping to shake off a negative headspace and motivate normalcy and social behaviour. Where one person may listen to sad songs when they're happy and happy songs when they're sad, the next might do the complete opposite, and this range is part of why music can be so effective in affecting our mood.

One study involving various kinds of auditory and visual treatments for depression stated that "Music-based interventions is an important nonpharmacological intervention used in the treatment of psychiatric and behavioral disorders, and the obvious curative effect on depression has been observed" (Tang et al., 2020, p. 2). However, one of the difficulties with music intervention is the range of available treatments and the difficulty in identifying causation from overlapping factors. That same study noted that "Music therapy is an established health profession in which music is used within a therapeutic relationship to address physical, emotional, cognitive, and social needs of individuals, and includes the triad of music, clients and qualified music therapists." This kind of treatment is similar to any other therapy session with the goal to improve things like mood, stress levels, and overall well-being. "Music medicine is defined as mainly listening to prerecorded music provided by medical personnel or rarely listening to live music." Applications of music medicine would be more in line with tackling physical pain or other general purposes. Music medicine is also a relatively new discipline with research only picking up within the last decade or so. In terms of results, they found that the most effective treatment at reducing depressive symptoms was music therapy that was supported by guided imagery. While research still needs to continue, these methods provide people with more options and combinations than standard therapy. It may also reduce the need for medications that often come with undesirable side effects and require accurate diagnosis and dosage.

The final mood disorder we'll look at is bipolar disorder which is "Made up of three different parts: depression, mania and normal feelings" (Canadian Mental Health Association, 2013). The distinguishing factor of bipolar disorder from the other mood disorders is the experience of mania. Bipolar disorder is often thought of as a person experiencing extreme high's and low's but this isn't necessarily the case since "Some people experience [mania] as feeling very happy, but others feel very irritable or angry." Furthermore, people are more likely to engage in reckless or risky behviour such as going on expensive shopping sprees, engaging in substance use or having risky sex. Some of the difficulty in diagnosing and treating bipolar comes from the fact that "Bipolar disorder can look different in each person depending on how long the mania and depression episodes last, how severe they are, how quickly a person's mood changes and how long a person has normal mood in between." For most people with bipolar disorder, it is a persisting condition that is often diagnosed in the late teens and early twenties but it can present itself at any point in life and exist alongside other conditions. Bipolar I is identified when a patient has "had at least one manic episode that may be preceded or followed by hypomanic or major depressive episodes. In some cases, mania may trigger a break from reality" (Mayo Clinic, 2021). Bipolar II is identified when a patient has, "had at least one major depressive episode and at least one hypomanic episode, but ... never had a manic episode." It's important to note that, "Bipolar II disorder is not a milder form of bipolar I disorder, but a separate diagnosis. While the manic episodes of bipolar I disorder can be severe and dangerous, individuals with bipolar II disorder can be depressed for longer periods, which can cause significant impairment." In terms of medications, there are several options to accommodate the variety of symptoms. Like with conditions previously discussed, antianxiety, antidepressants, and antipsychotics, are all possible treatment options. Mood stabilizers such as Eskalith that contain lithium carbonate have also proven to be effective at reducing the severity of manic episodes.

In a paper on analogous models, Angeler (2018) aimed to connect heavy metal music with mental illness. They explained that "Metal music consists of a variety of subgenres with distinct manifestations of song, rhythm, instrumentation, and vocal structure. These manifestations are analogous to the symptomatology of bipolar disorder, specifically the recurrent episodes of (hypo)mania and depression" (Angeler, 2018, p. 1). It is the smaller, more distinctive subgenres that are the focus of the analogies because they express the diversity in emotions those with bipolar disorder might experience during depressive or manic episodes. They drew further comparisons between the way society and different cultures view bipolar disorder and metal music. Since neither fit the mold of many cultural, religion, and ethical belief models, they are frequently stigmatized. In this light, metal music may be something that those suffering with mental illness could naturally gravitate towards, either for enjoyment or as inspiration. The study adds that these analogies, "May be useful for mental health literacy because they may metaphorically "mirror" the soul of the suffering patient. The lines of inquiry in this paper show that metal as an art form has potential to stimulate thinking about the complexity of mental illnesses" (Angeler, 2018, p. 8).

"It is not easy to accept a disability as part of one's identity, and more so when it is accompanied by stigma" (Sharma, 2014, p. 74). This stigma may not only postpone a person from seeking help, but could in some cases prevent them from doing so all together. This unfortunate truth was explored in an autoethnographic study where the author explores their path to recovery across many years of struggle. Music was crucial in this process but not in the same way as other medications or treatments. The author goes on to explain that their path to "Self-healing via music was largely accomplished because musical engagement was at an occupational level, not just a traditionally therapeutic one mediated by a therapist" (Sharma, 2014, p. 81). From this we can see that writing, teaching, and playing music can supply people with important tools that may enable us to work through difficult times, even when struggling with mental illness.

Chapter 2 References:

Angeler, D. G. (2018, April 5). Analogies between Heavy Metal Music and the Symptoms of

Mental Illness. Challenges (20781547), 9(1), 18. https://doi.org/10.3390/challe9010018

Burcusa, S. L., & Iacono, W. G. (2007, December). Risk for recurrence in depression. Clinical

psychology review, 27(8), 959–985. https://doi.org/10.1016/j.cpr.2007.02.005

Canadian Mental Health Association. (2013). Mood Disorders. CMHA British Columbia.

https://cmha.bc.ca/documents/mood-disorders-2/

Chen, X., Li, H., Zheng, X., & Huang, J. (2021, July 2). Effects of music therapy on COVID-19

patients' anxiety, depression, and life quality: A protocol for systematic review and meta-analysis. Medicine, 100(26), e26419. https://doi.org/10.1097/MD.000000000

0026419

Mayo Clinic. (2021, February 16). Bipolar disorder - Symptoms and causes. https://www.mayo

clinic.org/diseases-conditions/bipolar-disorder/symptoms-causes/syc-20355955

Panchal, N., Kamal, R., Cox, C., & Garfield, R. (2021, February 10). The Implications of

COVID-19 for Mental Health and Substance Use. KFF. https://www.kff.org/corona

virus-covid-19/issue-brief/the-implications-of-covid-19-for-mental-health-and-substance-

use/

Sharma, P. (2014). Making Song, Making Sanity: Recovery from Bipolar Disorder. Canadian

Journal of Music Therapy, 20(1), 65–84.

Tang, Q., Huang, Z., Zhou, H., & Ye, P. (2020, November 18). Effects of music therapy on

depression: A meta-analysis of randomized controlled trials. PloS One, 15(11), e0240862. https://doi.org/10.1371/journal.pone.0240862

World Health Organization. (2020, January 30). Depression. Retrieved from the WHO website:

https://www.who.int/en/news-room/fact-sheets/detail/depression

Chapter 3: Psychotic Disorders

In this chapter, we will discuss the intricacies of music in the context of people who experience psychosis and its accompanying illnesses, particularly schizophrenia, a complicated condition to both treat and live with. The Centre for Addiction and Mental Health (n.d.) presents psychosis as a term to describe conditions that affect the mind and its ability to distinguish between what is real and what is not. Positive symptoms are described as symptoms that add to or distort the person's normal functioning and can range from sensory hallucinations to non-sensory delusions or beliefs that may result in difficulty concentrating. Negative symptoms involve normal functioning becoming lost or reduced such as a diminished display of emotion and reduced motivation or social functioning which can make everyday tasks and interactions more difficult. These symptoms usually arise by a person's late teens or early twenties and while psychotic disorders aren't as common as other disorders, still "About three out of every 100 people will experience an episode of psychosis in their lifetime" (Centre for Addiction and Mental Health, n.d.). There is often difficulty in determining what the cause for a first episode is since psychosis occurs in a variety of mental and physical disorders. However, seeking treatment following the onset of symptoms, even as early as the first episode, strongly increases the chance of a favourable prognosis. One of these treatments is the intervention of medications like antipsychotics that are often necessary to maintain daily functioning and may be combined with other medications like antidepressants that also affect the balance of neurotransmitters in the brain to treat coinciding symptoms or conditions. Various other types of therapies are often involved alongside medications such as psychotherapy, counselling, as well as education about a patient's own experiences, symptoms, and lifestyle. It was presented that a combination of biological factors like someone's genetics can place a person at a higher risk of psychosis. However, a psychotic episode is often triggered by environmental factors like substance use and stress. Additionally, psychosis can be induced by head trauma and various other illnesses like multiple sclerosis, Alzheimer's disease, and Parkinson's disease.

Schizophrenia is labelled when, "A person has some psychotic symptoms for at least six months, with a significant decline in the ability to function" (Centre for Addiction and Mental Health, n.d.). As discussed, psychosis appears in a variety of different conditions beyond schizophrenia such as with schizoaffective disorder and bipolar disorder. Schizoaffective disorder is when, "A person will have symptoms of schizophrenia and, at some point in the course of illness, concurrent symptoms of a mood disturbance." Those with bipolar disorder however experience psychosis symptoms related more to mood disturbance than thought disturbance. While psychotic episodes may appear as little as once in some people's life, psychosis is recurrent in schizophrenia, a chronic condition that requires consistent maintenance in regards to its symptoms.

A tall hurdle for psychotic disorders is the stigma associated with it. This may be attributed to drug use, misrepresentation in media, and a lack of understanding and empathy towards the difficulties and challenges associated with disorders that affect mental health. Drug use results in an altered state of consciousness, and while the same can be said with the positive symptoms of schizophrenia, the nature of this state is different and still usually accompanied by negative symptoms. However, drug-induced psychosis is when, "The use of drugs such as cannabis, cocaine, ecstasy, ketamine, LSD, amphetamines and alcohol can sometimes cause psychotic symptoms" (Centre for Addiction and Mental Health, n.d.). This overlap can create a distorted perception of psychosis in people with psychotic disorders in damaging ways, for example, by associating the positive symptoms of schizophrenia with the hallucinatory effects of LSD. Drug induced psychosis also often goes away after cessation of the drug that caused it which contrasts the lifelong maintenance of many with schizophrenia.

Furthermore, the way positive symptoms are portrayed and broadcast in the media has also had a serious impact on the public view of these conditions. Oftentimes, the nature and severity of hallucinations and delusions has been dangerously exaggerated while more common symptoms like social withdrawal, reduced expression, and hindered motivation are underplayed. As well as misrepresentation, displays of violence within portrayals of mental illness in film and television are dangerous contributors to the stigma of it. Lastly, schizophrenia most commonly appears in early adulthood and is more common in males than in females. Males are also more likely to have a difficult time dealing with mental health issues than their female counterparts due to factors like societal pressures, a lack of support circles, and less effective coping behaviours. In fact, "The rate of suicide is highest in middle-aged white men" (American Foundation for Suicide Prevention, 2021). This shows the effects of the current barriers for men in dealing with their mental health and an unfortunate result is an increase of these men ending up in areas like rehabilitation centres and homeless shelters. The presence of people with psychotic disorders in these populations in turn contributes to the stigma around mental health due to how the majority of the public perceive these groups. Lastly, while psychotic disorders, substance abuse, and suicide rates may be statistically higher in men, complications with mental health can happen to anybody.

The first study we'll discuss takes a look at how "Mental health patients with a diagnosis of psychosis experienced participation in music therapy, in general, and more specifically how they experienced music therapy in relation to their current mental state and life situation (Solli, 2015, p. 67). The participants were interviewed about their experience with the treatment in various mediums such as in group settings or individually. Over the last few years, there has been an increased focus and value on the perspectives of those dealing with mental health difficulties and their experiences with treatment. A prominent finding within this study was that music therapy was experienced as enjoyable and participants were more engaged with therapy and motivated. This is significant because psychotic illnesses like schizophrenia are generally characterized by a lack of motivation and apathy and throughout the various delivery methods, "Music therapy made them feel more vital, uplifted, joyful, hopeful, and motivated, and enabled them to become more active participants in their everyday lives" (Solli, 2015, p. 83).

While there isn't necessarily a decrease in the negative symptoms of schizophrenia, there is still an overall increase in well-being and function. The music intervention doesn't reverse an ailment or a condition but rather makes the existing complication more manageable. Solli (2015, p. 83) suggests that music therapy was effective in regaining a patients sense of self, identity, and aliveness because of the connection our taste and love of music is to our identity and sense of self. People who develop schizophrenia often lose this consequently experience difficulties with communicating and maintaining important relationships with others and themselves. For example, people who are non-verbal due to schizophrenia may be able to engage in social behaviour through actively contributing in group musical sessions either by playing or just by listening to music. While many found music therapy to be helpful, "several of the participants did not consider music therapy to be a treatment, instead emphasizing its representation of freedom from illness, stigma, and treatment" (Solli, 2015, p. 84). It appears that an important aspect of utilizing music for therapy is the very fact that it isn't just another doctor appointment or prescription to patients. Implementing it into clinical settings may actually have an adverse effect on a patient's perception of the experience since the personal connection and sense of freedom was what made music so effective in this group in the first place.

In studies on the effect of background music on working attention in people with schizophrenia, it was found that "Background music in the workplace should focus mainly on building an environment in which listeners feel loved and safe, and avoiding music that causes individuals to feel stressed or sad" (Shih et al., 2016, as cited in Shih et al., 2020, p. 120). It was also noted that background music tended to increase attention scores in persons with schizophrenia to a significant statistical degree. While more studies have to replicate these results, this finding is interesting because background music frequently acts as a distraction for people without psychotic disorders and tends to lower their ability to perform attention based tasks requiring focus and concentration. In most cases, sung melodies accompanied by words make us want to sing, follow along, or otherwise attend to the music instead of a task. For these reasons, instrumental or non-vocal music may be a better alternative for tasks like work or studying but the absence of music is likely still better. However, in people with schizophrenia, auditory hallucinations can be incredibly distracting and popular music with lyrics may actually be grounding to the person and help to block out hallucinations. This stands as a reminder of how important it is to consider the range of mental health and personal experiences that can affect how people respond to different stimuli or treatment.

Chapter 3 References:

American Foundation for Suicide Prevention. (2021, September 9). Suicide statistics.

https://afsp.org/suicide-statistics/

Centre for Addiction and Mental Health. (n.d.). Psychosis. CAMH. Retrieved August 27, 2021,

from https://www.camh.ca/en/health-info/mental-illness-and-addiction-in-dex/psychosis

Shih, Y. N., Chen, C. S., Chiang, H. Y., & Liu, C.H. (2015). Influence of background music on work attention in clients with chronic schizophrenia. Work, 51(1),

153–158. https://doi.org/10.3233/wor-141846

Shih, Y. N., Chu, K. H., & Wu, C. C. (2020). The effects of background music tempo on the

work attention performance of workers with schizophrenia. Work, 66(1), 119–123.

https://doi.org/10.3233/WOR-203156

Solli, H. P., & Rolvsjord, R. (2015). "The Opposite of Treatment": A qualitative study of how

patients diagnosed with psychosis experience music therapy. Nordic Journal of Music

Therapy, 24(1), 67–92. https://doi.org/10.1080/08098131.2014.890639

Chapter 4: PTSD

According to Statistics Canada (2012), "Post traumatic stress disorder (PTSD) is a disorder caused by a traumatic event that is outside the normal realm of human experience, such as rape, assault, torture, being kidnapped or held captive, military combat, severe car accidents, and natural or manmade disasters." While the nature of the traumatic incident can differ, they can result in intense fear, hopelessness, and horror from real or threatened physical harm to one's self or others. The intensity and duration of the incident may also impact the severity of the resulting PTSD, especially if the traumatic event was unexpected. In general, emotional impairment is a result of guilt, anxiety, depression, difficulty sleeping or concentrating, and recurrent flashbacks. Statistics Canada (2012) continues that flashbacks or nightmares caused by traumatic incidents may be caused or triggered by ordinary occurrences and can feel as if the individual was reliving the situation. Women are statistically more likely to develop PTSD than men, likely due to the increased rate of intimate partner violence against them, however, it can develop in anyone at any age and be chronic in nature. In most cases, symptoms last at least a month and begin within three months of the traumatic event. Unlike other anxiety disorders, the source of the illness is usually obvious and approximately half of those who suffer with PTSD will fully recover within three to six months. Unfortunately, some can experience symptoms for years or never fully recover.

In general, "PTSD is diagnosed based on six criteria" (Statistics Canada, 2012). Statistics Canada (2012) describes the first as the initial traumatizing incident that elicits a response of intense fear or horror as a result of real or threatened injury to themselves or others. Secondly, the individual re-experiences the event in various forms of recurrent and invasive thoughts, flashbacks, or dreams as a result of exposure to cues that resemble an aspect of the event. The third criteria is avoidance behaviour of any activities, places, or people that may bring back thoughts or feelings of the trauma. This can result in feelings of detachment or estrangement from others as well as a restricted ability to feel emotions, engage in intimacy, or look to the future. Fourth, persistent symptoms of arousal may cause insomnia, irritability, and difficulty concentrating as a result of the hypervigilance, and/or exaggerated startle response. The symptoms remaining present for more than a month is the fifth diagnosis criteria. The final criteria is symptoms causing clinically significant impairments to social, occupational, or other areas of functioning. For individuals suffering with PTSD, "Early diagnosis … is essential to improve prognosis [as] individuals who remain ill one year after the traumatic event rarely recover completely" (Statistics Canada, 2012).

As far as standard medical treatment goes, selective serotonin reuptake inhibitors or SSRIs are the standard first-line of treatment, especially for long term use in those with chronic PTSD. Statistics Canada (2012) continues that other antidepressants like tricyclic antidepressants and tranquilizers known as benzodiazepines can also be used to great effect. The aim of all PTSD treatments is for the full remission of symptoms and so it's important that any medications being used are safe for extended periods of time. Alongside medication, psychotherapies like cognitive-behavioural therapy that focus on identifying and changing harmful thought patterns can also help to overcome the symptoms of PTSD.

One study found "significant changes of trauma symptoms, well-being and sleep quality" (Beck et al., 2018) in traumatized refugees while implementing a music therapy method called Trauma-focused Music and Imagery (TMI). This method is an adaptation of another called Guided Imagery and Music (GIM) which involves listening to classical music in an altered state of consciousness as a therapeutic medium. According to Beck et al. (2018), a typical TMI session begins with verbal confirmations to check in about the persisting issues and the overall focus for the music listening. One key difference between TMI and GIM is the choice in music. While GIM uses predominantly western classical music, TMI has a greater focus on the patients needs and the music can thus be chosen by either the patient or the therapist from a wide range of genres beyond just classical music. Some of these might include film, meditative, or cultural music but anything the patient and practitioner find appropriate can work. Furthermore, the patient can position themselves as they wish to aid with the guided relaxation, mindful breathing, and focus on one's inner image that comes at the beginning of the session. The music listening aspect then begins with the therapist being able to guide the participant through the music or just back to the present at the end of the set. The patient then draws an image that can be discussed in context of the experience and overall meaningfulness of the therapeutic process. Finally, assigned homework in the form of listening, journaling, or otherwise may be provided as needed.

This study used a randomized parallel-group design with two intervention groups with the first being a TMI music group and the second being a standard verbal psychological treatment group with the main goal to compare results and efficacy between the groups. The point of verbal guidance in the music listening group is to "[support] the deepening and integration of the ongoing stream of imagery, emotions and sensations evoked by the music" (Beck et al., 2018). On the other hand, the standard psychological treatment group was built off of, "a broad range of theoretical models such as narrative therapy, cognitive therapy, social psychology and neuro-affective therapy." Measurements were taken at baseline, post therapy, and at a six month follow up with client evaluation also being collected after each session.

Trauma interrupts autonomic regulation with increased sympathetic and para-sympathetic responses known as fight or flight in the former and freeze or feign in the latter. Beck et al. (2018) present that, "PTSD is connected to stress-re-lated loss of hippocampal mass and hypervigilance related to an increased amygdala-hippocampus connectivity." Brain studies on music's effect on this suggest that music's ability to enhance the connection between the amygdala/hippocampus regions with the prefrontal areas can reduce the hypervigilance and increase the cognitive processing of emotion. Furthermore, a functional magnetic resonance imaging (fMRI) study found that GIM was more effective than guided imagery, isolated music, and a control group at recalling and pro-cessing episodic and traumatic memories associated with negative emotions. One reason may be that, "Calm music and speaking combined with a thor-ough attunement to the patient might activate the social engagement system, lead to down-regulation of arousal, and enable the patient to unfreeze and experience aliveness and energy."

A 9% prevalence of PTSD was found amongst adult refugees in a systematic review of 20 surveys collected across 7 different countries. That number is ap-proximately 10 times the rates in the age-matched populations of those same countries. This group is not only more likely to be exposed to traumatizing events, but they are often less likely to seek or find the support they need once they've escaped a volatile environment. When considering that individuals who go untreated for over a year rarely fully recover, it's understandable that this demographic has such a high prevalence of PTSD compared to those of a similar age bracket in the same countries. In response to this complexity, the researchers suggest that, "other measures than the level of trauma symptoms have to be recognized when evaluating the effect of specific therapies in this patient group" (Beck et al., 2018). The wishful effect of this particular study is for GIM and other alternative therapies to be considered in ultimately expand-ing treatment and improving refugee health and integration.

In supporting music in PTSD therapy, two Australian school studies found a decrease in hyperactivity, aggressive behaviour, depression, and anxiety among 31 new refugees when engaged in music therapy. Furthermore, various studies seem to support music therapy in those with PTSD with another con-cluding that, "individual and group interventions seem to reduce core PTSD symptoms and depression and increase social function, hope and resilience in both adults and children" (Beck et al., 2018). The adults in this study were all unable to benefit from cognitive behavioural therapy (CBT) yet displayed a de-crease in all aspects of PTSD symptomatology following group music impro-visation when compared to a control. For the kids, aged 9-17 with histories of sexual abuse, group music therapy showed some effect at reducing symptoms just after four songwriting sessions. One of the best parts about music therapy is that it offers a safe space to young people and can provide a way to address issues and needs in verbal and non-verbal ways. This method of interaction and communication may be more effective in children since "Verbal therapy used in isolation is often met with resistance by victims of sexual abuse because their abuser or other trusted adults used words to lie to, threaten, or mislead them" (Rogers, 1995, as cited in Eyre, 2013). This can then be a way to rebuild that trust with the therapist and ultimately facilitate the transition from childhood to adulthood. Therapists in this setting have a lot of responsibility and must be prepared to relive unthinkable experiences alongside the patient in order to reach the core of their trauma. A final study involving ten women with histories of sexual and or physical childhood abuse found a significant degree of symptom relief from PTSD symptoms as well as dissociation, anxiety, and depression as a result of trauma-focused group GIM.

Music therapy in the treatment of trauma can help "build up inner resources in the patient necessary for working through the trauma story, such as positive memories, a feeling of strength, a safe place, or the aesthetic experience of music" (Beck et al., 2018). It can also help in the recollection and narration of traumatic episodes by providing a structured framework that can prevent the patient from getting stuck in a repetitive flashback or from fragmenting their story. This can play a significant part in dismantling a troubling response to potentially triggering events and it seems that the reframing of imagery or experiences is improved when a patient's imagination is involved. New solutions or perspectives to a traumatic episode can be gained in this way as well as the transformation of these memories into something formative and productive towards recovery.

Unfortunately, traumatization is a part of the human experience and "catastrophic event[s] (whether caused by an act of nature or a human) can overwhelm our ability to cope, resulting in a range of post-traumatic responses" (Eyre, 2013). In treating these, music therapy has seen an increase in popularity for multiple reasons, including the lack of side effects and risks that so often come with medical treatment. While this is true in most cases, it's possible that certain artists, songs, or sounds, including those involved in music production, could serve as a potential trigger for those suffering from PTSD despite the best intentions of a therapist or health care provider. This doesn't mean music therapy shouldn't be considered or used, but communication, care, and awareness must be maintained in order to put the patients well-being first.

Chapter 4 References:

Beck, B. D., Lund, S. T., Søgaard, U., Simonsen, E., Tellier, T. C., Cordtz, T. O., Laier, G. H., &

Moe, T. (2018). Music therapy versus treatment as usual for refugees diagnosed with

posttraumatic stress disorder (PTSD): study protocol for a randomized controlled trial.

Trials, 19(1). https://doi.org/10.1186/s13063-018-2662-z

Eyre, L. (2013). Guidelines for Music Therapy Practice in Mental Health. Barcelona Publishers.

Statistics Canada. (2012, January 30). Section B - Anxiety disorders. https://www150.statcan.

gc.ca/n1/pub/82-619-m/2012004/sections/sectionb-eng.htm#archived

Chapter 5: ADHD

According to Statistic Canada (2012), "Attention-deficit/hyperactivity disorder (ADHD) is characterized by inattention, hyperactivity and impulsivity, and is one of the most common mental health conditions in children." In this case, boys are statistically three times more likely than girls to develop ADHD. While it is often categorized as a childhood condition due to symptoms frequently becoming noticeable or prevalent during the early years of education, there are still cases where adults are diagnosed with ADHD and many of these people will have lived the majority of their lives with untreated symptoms. In cases where a child is diagnosed, roughly three quarters will persist throughout adolescence and over half into adulthood. The severity of childhood cases and degree of treatments has also been found to predict adult ADHD.

There are three main types of diagnosis of ADHD presented by Statistics Canada (2012), predominantly inattentive type, predominantly hyperactive-impulsive type, and combined type. The first type is diagnosed in the presence of, "Six or more of the following symptoms of inattention: often pays little attention to details or makes careless mistakes in school/work; has difficulty staying attentive in tasks or activities; seems not to listen when spoken to directly; fails to finish a task or does not follow through on instructions; often has difficulty with organizing tasks and activities; either avoids, dislikes, or is reluctant to partake in tasks that require sustained effort (e.g., schoolwork, homework); often misplaces items that are required for tasks or activities; is easily distracted by external stimuli; and/or is often forgetful in daily activities."

Predominantly hyperactive-impulsive type is diagnosed if they have, Six or more of the following symptoms of hyperactivity or impulsivity: often fidgets or squirms; often leaves seat/chair when remaining seated is expected; often runs around in inappropriate situations; has difficulty playing quietly; is often "on the go"; often talks excessively; often blurts out answers to questions that have not been completed; has difficulty waiting their turn; or often interrupts/intrudes others. (Statistics Canada, 2012)

The final diagnosis, ADHD-combined type, is when a patient experiences six symptoms from inattentive type and six from hyperactive-impulsive type. In regards to ADHD-combined type, the defining symptoms include, "inattention, hyperactivity and impulsivity."

The above symptoms may explain the frequency at which parents and teachers suspect children of having ADHD. The reason being that most children at one point or another have displayed at least one of, if not multiple, instances of these behaviours. As such, ADHD remains one of the most commonly overdiagnosed conditions in children. The effects of a misdiagnosis can have drastic effects on a developing adolescent from self esteem issues to side effects from medications that they don't need. In order to prevent this, we have already seen that accurate diagnosis requires at least six or more of the listed behaviours be present. Additionally, these symptoms, "must have been present before seven years of age, and some impairment must be shown in at least two settings (e.g., school, home)" (Statistic Canada, 2012). Lastly, the present symptoms must clearly impact social, academic, or occupational functioning and not be the result of comorbidity with another disorder. While there has been significant research done on ADHD, it is still unclear as to what directly causes it. A combination of genetics, home environments, and other factors like premature birth, lead exposure, injury, or maternal use of drugs, tobacco, or alcohol could be responsible. It has also been theorized that developmental failure in the brain could result in the impairment of self-control and inhibition found in ADHD.

A combination of medication, therapy, and counseling is currently considered the most effective treatment for ADHD by Statistics Canada (2012). The aim of psychotherapy is to address and learn new behaviours that will help people deal with the emotional effects of ADHD and ultimately raise their self esteem. For medication, "Ritalin (a short-acting methylphenidate) is the most common medication and helps to reduce hyperactivity and improve the ability to focus, work and learn. It's discussed that two of the most common side effects of this drug are insomnia and appetite suppression. Other medications with similar effects include dextroamphetamine (Dexadrine or Dextrostat), pemoline (Cylert) and Adderall." It's important to note that medications such as these shouldn't be taken indefinitely and the discontinuation of them is often a way to assess or reassess a child's condition.

The worldwide prevalence of ADHD is approximately 5-10% making it "one of the most common mental disorders during childhood and adolescence" (Madjar et al., 2020). Due to ADHD often appearing in such formative years of a person's personal and academic life, the effects can have a significant impact on development and if left unmanaged, could lead to a higher risk of dropping out, substance abuse, and unemployment as they transition to adulthood. Madjar et al. (2020) go on to present that research in this area is important to identify optimal settings for learning to properly support children and adolescents with ADHD.

Brenden Hiebert

When considering the effects of music listening on non-ADHD people, it's generally accepted that it mostly becomes a distraction that affects reading ability and limits learning processes. However research completed by Madjar et al. (2020) suggest that calm music may actually help those with ADHD to better regulate their autonomous responses and enhance performance. In fact this study "aimed to explore particular settings that might optimize the performance of preadolescents with ADHD on academic tasks by integrating a conceptual framework of attention ... with previously established insights regarding the differences of autonomous nervous system (ANS) regulation between individuals with and without ADHD." An important aspect of this study is the load theory of selective attention. It's explained that maintaining attention in a given task is a balance between a conscious and goal-directed choice of a target stimulus (early-selection) and attention which is directed involuntarily toward a dominant stimulus (late-selection). This is important to the conceptual framework discussed earlier because cognitive resources are limited. Simply, as the perceptual load of the given task increases, the less likely it is that irrelevant stimuli are perceived. It was also suggested that children with ADHD had a harder time initiating the inhibition process should the distracting or late-selection stimulus be attended to. Adults with ADHD were also found to be distracted easier by irrelevant stimuli than those without it; however both groups showed benefit from tasks that reduced interference and distraction from a primary stimulus.

The study began with inviting volunteers with children who had an established ADHD diagnosis without any comorbid disorders. The performance of these participants was measured in the context of a reading comprehension task designed to explore the relationship between late-selection mechanisms and optimal perceptual load on inhibition capacity. The research team made three hypotheses in their study. The first being that "reading with background music would improve the comprehension of preadolescents with ADHD and impair the performance of typically developed peers" (Madjar et al., 2020). The results supported this hypothesis with calming music having the largest effect compared to more arousing or rhythmic music.

It was suggested that background music might increase the load of the late-selection mechanism related to the given task which would then limit the person's ability to direct their attention to an irrelevant stimulus. Due to a difference in attentional capacity, children were less distracted by high perceptual loads compared to adults since the background stimulus would not be processed or noticed by children. Since external stimuli often easily distract those with ADHD, monotonous and persistent stimuli are better for activating the late-selection mechanisms.

The second hypothesis stated that "Preadolescents with ADHD would have a smaller decrease in mean-levels of [heart rate variability] under background music conditions compared with typically developed peers." Heart rate variability was used in this study to effectively measure the effect music had on the participants. In other words, those that were positively affected by music and scored better in reading comprehension tasks would be indicated by less of a decrease in heart rate variability where those who were negatively affected by music and scored worse in reading comprehension would be indicated by a greater decrease in heart rate variability. In fact, for people with ADHD, there was very little decline in HRV during exposure to music, indicating fewer demands on the autonomous nervous system. In contrast, for those without ADHD, there was a steady decline in HRV, indicating higher arousal of the ANS when listening to music. These findings are in support of their second claim.

The third and final hypothesis presented was that "Participants with [a] smaller decrease of mean-levels [of] HRV under music conditions would improve their performance compared [to] those with [a] higher decrease of mean-levels of HRV (regardless of ADHD diagnosis)." The results again backed up the hypothesis that those who were positively affected by the music (smaller decrease in HRV), were the same who benefited most from listening to it while reading. It's important to note that particular differences between music types were not the focus of this study. Three different types were used but no relevant empirical data was collected.

One of the previous research findings considered in this study was that "Listening to music can have a substantial impact on the [autonomic nervous system] under certain conditions" (Madjar et al., 2020). The given example was that of a professional singer's heart rate and respiration falling in line with the music they were listening to. The effect is music specific and this alignment was not found in meaningless sounds or while listening during physical activity. Another finding that informed the design of the study was that "substantial difficulties in reading comprehension are prevalent among adolescents with ADHD." This of course isn't the only academic task that can cause excessive difficulty for those with ADHD but it was deemed successfully testable by the researchers and was integrated as the main grounds for testing. This study also aimed to focus on the cognitive differences between those with ADHD and those without it instead of focusing on just the difference in emotional responses between the groups.

One of the most important outcomes for this study is that the results challenge the standard thought that ADHD students or individuals exclusively need quiet settings to focus and work effectively. It may shed light on ways that teachers, practitioners, and others can support those with ADHD with intuitive approaches and case by case solutions instead of a generalized blanket approach for all people. Besides avoiding unwanted side effects, this form of treatment is likely already accessible for most families since background music listening doesn't require expensive equipment or tools. It also doesn't need trained professionals to be used at home or in classrooms and "may improve the learning experience of numerous adolescents who struggle with attention deficits daily and initiate novel approach[es] in future research on scholastic interventions for ADHD" (Madjar et al., 2020).

At the very least, listening to music is a harm free option that may improve the way those with ADHD approach studying and other environments that they have difficulty in. While the results suggest that music is likely to distract or decrease productivity in most people without ADHD, for some it may still be a force that keeps them at their desk similar to that of a cup of coffee. Slowly but consistently working through a difficult task is still better than not doing it at all.

Chapter 5 References:
Madjar, N., Gazoli, R., Manor, I., & Shoval, G. (2020). Contrasting effects of music on reading comprehension in preadolescents with and without ADHD. Psychiatry Research, 291. https://doi.org/10.1016/j.psychres.2020.113207
Statistics Canada. (2012, January 30). Section C - Childhood conditions. Retrieved May 20, 2022, from https://www150.statcan.gc.ca/n1/pub/82-619-m/2012004/sections/sectionc-eng.htm#a1

Chapter 6: Brain Injury

Brain injury is one of the highest reported injuries in Canada due to the prevalence of concussions, strokes, and tumours or cancers. In fact, "By 2031, traumatic brain injury (TBI) is expected to be among the most common neurological conditions affecting Canadians" (Brain Injury Canada, n.d.). Sports like hockey and ringette are some of the leading causes for concussions in youth, while falls are largely responsible for brain injury in the elderly. Recurrent or severe head trauma has been, "identified as a risk factor for Alzheimer's disease and other dementias in men, and for epilepsy in both sexes." Traumatic brain injury may also share a link with Parkinson's disease, a neurological condition that the boxing legend Muhammad Ali famously endured throughout the later half of his life. Indeed, "[a] significant proportion (5–7%) of patients with MTBI [mild traumatic brain injury] present a later cognitive decline" (Balzani et al., 2014).

The mechanism and location of injury plays a big part in the severity, duration, and prognosis of the sustained injury. For concussions, the brain is suspended in spinal fluid that protects and maintains it, however, with enough force the brain can compress or make contact with the skull, leading to injury. For a stroke, the brain cells in the affected area are either damaged or killed leading to injury and a lack of functionality in the affected area. Fortunately, the brain is able to compensate for these lost parts and share responsibilities across different regions to a certain degree. Lastly, removing malignant or benign tumours can sometimes lead to complications or developments beyond the average expected danger of the growth as with surgery or chemotherapy.

Some of the most common symptoms of brain injury include confusion, nausea, headaches, vertigo, and even seizures. It's important to seek medical attention following an injury to the head to identify any life threatening conditions such as a cerebral edema or swelling of the brain, which can be fatal. In regards to head trauma, post concussion syndrome or PCS is the most common experience following an accident or injury involving a concussion and is what persists following the incident. These lasting symptoms often include dizziness, headaches, and difficulty with memory and concentrating. This can be incredibly impactful on youth, especially in a classroom setting where kids may already find it difficult to stay focused for extended periods of time without dealing with an injury. In the context of musical tasks, "PCS is both an organic and a psychological syndrome that impairs subjectivity and historicity of the subjects, making these patients, whose brains are morphologically intact, partially disabled, because music listening, time perception, and continuity of thoughts involve very complex cognitive processes required in everyday life."

Despite the prevalence of neurological, behavioural, and psychological change following injury to the brain, "our lack of knowledge of these conditions can hamper the rehabilitation and ... professional reintegration of these individuals for many years after their accident" (Guétin et al., 2009). Unlike other injuries, our equipment isn't always capable of detecting or identifying injury. While an MRI (magnetic resonance imaging) scan can detect moderate to severe injury, mild concussions often don't display results that can be observed or measured in the same way an X-Ray might for a broken bone. Another tool, the fMRI (function magnetic resonance imaging) that measures changes in blood flow has enabled researchers to study how various treatments may affect an individual with traumatic brain injury, including the relationship music has with cognitive and cerebral functioning in these individuals.

Some studies suggest that for this demographic, "music therapy stimulates cognitive functions, acts on anxiety, depressive phases and aggressiveness and thus significantly improves mood, communication and independence in brain-injured patients" (Guétin et al., 2009). It was observed that active therapy or simply playing with instruments and engaging in music-making stimulated psychomotor and cognitive functions such as coordination and concentration while receptive therapy or listening based treatment targeted improvement in mood and anxiety while also encouraging expression of symptoms. Music therapy may not be effective on all aspects of recovery for those with traumatic brain injury, but it is easy to include in a treatment program and it may still prove valuable and effective in areas associated with memory, mood, and behaviour as discussed earlier. One of the reasons that the receptive music therapy may be effective is because "individualized musical listening markedly relieves painful experiences." It does so through various interacting sensory, cognitive, and behavioural mechanisms where repeated use can have long term effects in all of these areas.

An under-discussed aspect of mild and severe TBI is that there appears to be "a global change in music listening, mainly consisting of a reduction in listening, noise intolerance, and a decrease in pleasure or immersive feelings in music" (Balzani et al., 2014). This extends into PCS where there is a persistent reduction in the ability to engage in music listening and making. This, of course, appears contradictory to the claims regarding music therapy in treatment for those with brain injury. While there has been research in the areas where it may be beneficial such as with neurological and psychiatric disease, "the scientific literature exploring changes in the quality of music listening is sparse" (Balzani et al., 2014). It very well may be a two sided coin and even more complicated for working musicians.

As discussed, a decrease in tolerance to loud noises on its own significantly impacts almost every musician regardless of their role. For performers, band re-hearsals become extra taxing especially when considering the need to stand and endure a drummer's playing for hours on end. The sound techs also perform alongside musicians and have to stand and work in a loud club for the duration of a night. For those involved in production, music must be worked on at a rela-tively loud level (approximately 85-90 dB SPL) to ensure even perception of the frequency spectrum for accurate decision making. This may go on for multiple hours under normal circumstances. Combine this with general confusion, head-aches, and tiredness, and there's no doubt that both studio and live musicians and technicians would find their work interrupted by the effects of TBI.

Chapter 6 References:
Balzani, C., Mariaud, A.-S., Schön, D., Cermolacce, M., & Vion-Dury, J. (2014). Changes in
music listening in post-concussion syndrome after mild traumatic brain injury. Psychomusicology: Music, Mind, and Brain, 24(2), 117–124. https://doi.org/10.1037/pmu
0000037
Brain Injury Canada. (n.d.). Statistics on brain injury in Canada. Retrieved June 2, 2022, from
https://www.braininjurycanada.ca/en/statistics-brain-injury#:%7E:text=There%20are%20
200%2C000%20concussions%20annually,provide%20a%20diagnosis%20of%20concussion.
Guétin, S., Soua, B., Voiriot, G., Picot, M.-C., & Hérisson, C. (2009). The effect of music
therapy on mood and anxiety–depression: An observational study in institu-tionalised
patients with traumatic brain injury. Annals of Physical & Rehabilitation Med-icine, 52(1),
30–40. https://doi.org/10.1016/j.annrmp.2008.08.009

Chapter 7: Alzheimer's Disease

Alzheimer's disease is a form of dementia that affects 44 million people worldwide according to the Alzheimer's Association (n.d.). This number is greater than the entire population of Canada and reflects a disease that affects people all around the globe. Alzheimer's disease is also the most common type of dementia which is a term for a condition or state that affects mental processes due to injury, disease, or other means. While there are various forms of dementia, they all refer to a decrease or decay in brain function that is mostly, if not entirely, irreversible. For this reason alone, early diagnosis can be crucial in postponing the decline of functioning. For Alzheimer's, the expected life expectancy following the onset of symptoms appears to be approximately 8 years; however, the course of the disease will often vary between people. This can be due to differences in lifestyle, overall health, and current treatment plans. The symptoms most commonly associated with Alzheimer's are the decline in memory and overall cognition along with symptoms consistent with other dementias such as, "memory loss, difficulty performing daily activities, and changes in judgment, reasoning, behaviour and emotions" (Alzheimer Society of Canada, 2016). While there is no current cure for Alzheimer's disease, there are treatments and medications available that, alongside lifestyle changes and other treatments, can slow it down. However, everyone reacts differently to various treatments, including medications.

The Alzheimer's Society of Canada (2016) presents Alzheimer's disease as, "a disease of the brain where abnormal proteins collect in brain cells." Deposits of A-beta proteins block signals and clumps of Tau proteins tangle inside of neurons and cut off nutrients. These proteins ultimately result in the death of brain cells in those with Alzheimer's disease and are responsible for the progression of the disease. The onset of the disease isn't always clear although the greatest risk factor appears to be aging as the majority of Alzheimer's symptoms appear around 60 years of age. It is likely that a combination of our environment, history, lifestyle, and genetic makeup also contribute to the development of this disease. However, it should be noted that inherited Alzheimer's accounts for "less than 5% of all cases" (Alzheimer Society of Canada, 2016). This kind of Alzheimer's can develop at any age and is mostly related to the genetics of the person instead of their environment and lifestyle. Other conditions like Down Syndrome also seem to significantly increase the risk of developing Alzheimer's.

For a person with Alzheimer's or other kinds of dementia, the loss of memory can be distressing and lead to changes in personality and one's overall sense of self. This can be particularly difficult to deal with and it can make caring for and supporting these people more difficult because of how isolating and scary it can be. However, the areas of the brain that are responsible for musical behavior and memory are, "very often preserved in persons with dementia" (Eyre, 2013). This provides care takers, family members, and the patient with a connection to who that person may have been prior to the disease, but this phenomena goes beyond just an emotional connection and even impacts behaviour. In patients with later stage Alzheimer's, it's common for the person to lose the ability to speak or communicate almost entirely. Yet, in the presence of a familiar or favorable song, they can miraculously mouth, hum, or even sing along to the song with clear signs of rhythm and recognition. Beyond minimizing emotional distress, this could easily be integrated into therapy sessions for these patients.

One study found that various forms of music therapy, "improved some cognitive, psychological, and behavioural alterations in patients with [Alzheimer's Disease]" (Gomez et al., 2017). Notably, only 4 music therapy sessions were required for an effect on cognitive measures to be noticeable and appreciable in this case. While this was only one sample, it's reassuring evidence that music therapy may have a place in serious clinical treatment. One of the advantages of this kind of help is that there are various approaches that a practitioner or care taker could take to integrate music in therapy. Depending on the progression of the disease, the level of involvement and active participation can be adjusted accordingly to suit the abilities and needs of individual patients. This kind of therapy could range from group songwriting or instrument engagement to individual preferential listening sessions. Their own responses and attitudes towards the various approaches can also be used to guide the choice of activity or level of integration to ensure not only effective treatment but also well-being in the patient.

A recurrent point with the onset and course of Alzheimer's disease is that a healthy lifestyle can significantly reduce the chances of it developing in the first place as well as slowing the progression of the disease. One aspect of this is a person's physical health regarding things like their physical activity, diet, and substance use. The other aspect is a person's mental health that includes one's emotional state and mental exercise to maintain one's mental functioning. Anybody who has tried learning an instrument knows that music involves complex thought and coordination in order to create and play music. Most cases of music making involve some degree of lateralization or cross-talk between different hemispheres in the brain such as with hand independence when playing instruments like the guitar or piano. As we can see, music may serve as effective mental exercise while still being engaging, familiar, and potentially more enjoyable than standard treatments.

Brenden Hiebert

Chapter 7 References:

Alzheimer's Association. (n.d.). Alzheimer's & Dementia Help | Canada. Retrieved June 5,
2022, from https://www.alz.org/ca/dementia-alzheimers-canada.asp
Alzheimer Society of Canada. (2016, June). National resource library. Retrieved June 5, 2022,
from https://alzheimer.ca/en/help-support/dementia-resources/national-resource-library
Eyre, L. (2013). Guidelines for Music Therapy Practice in Mental Health. Barcelona Publishers.
Gómez Gallego, M., & Gómez García, J. (2017). Music therapy and Alzheimer's disease:
Cognitive, psychological, and behavioural effects. Neurología (English Edition), 32(5),
300–308. https://doi.org/10.1016/j.nrleng.2015.12.001

Chapter 8: Parkinson's Disease

Parkinson's disease is the second most common neurodegenerative disorder after Alzheimer's disease. Statistics suggest that for those over the age of 60, around 1 in 200 people will develop Parkinson's (Thompson, 2014). Thompson goes on to explain that the condition appears to be a result of degeneration in the substantia nigra, a part of the midbrain that is responsible for supplying the neurotransmitter dopamine to the basal ganglia. The basal ganglia is responsible for important motor functions like overall control, learning, as well as certain behaviours involving emotion, habits, and reward response. When there is an imbalance of neurotransmitters like dopamine, the function of the basal ganglia appears impaired and in the case of Parkinson's disease, the most noticeable symptoms are indeed motor problems. Some of these include, "tremors, [or] poorly timed movements including those involved in walking, impaired speech, and reduced facial expressions" (Thompson, 2014). They start off mild in the early stages of the disease and progressively get worse as it enters the later stages.

The relationship between Parkinson's disease and music is interesting and also promising from a music therapy standpoint. The phenomena known as rhythmic entrainment is likely the main mechanism to focus on according to Thompson (2014). It refers to the way that timing and rhythmic cues in music or other mediums substitute or compensate for the body's inability to correctly time and coordinate movements and actions, both simple and complex. By listening and following music, those with Parkinson's can be enabled to walk and even dance in ways they otherwise wouldn't be able to on their own. It's important to note that while the results can be drastic for some people, not everybody is affected to the same extent and individual responses to different kinds of music or movements can differ between individuals. This may be due to genetics, environment, experience, or a complex combination of the three. Non-musical sources of rhythmic stimulation like rhythmic beeps can also be used to a similar effect but music often comes with muscle memory that's associated with trained or rehearsed movements. Ballroom dancing, for example, could then be easier to replicate while listening to a waltz than with a series of mechanical beeps. The largest benefit of this phenomenon is that the improvements can be observed with little to no intervention or involvement from a dedicated music therapist or practitioner and can be done from anywhere.

In a study investigating the effect of music listening on brain activity in patients with Parkinson's disease, Maggioni et al. (2021) were able to reach several conclusions based on their findings. Firstly, they concluded that simple music listening on its own, "was not able to entirely compensate for the abnormal sensorimotor connectivity characterizing [Parkinson's disease] patients at rest" (Maggioni et al., 2021). This suggests that the external stimulus isn't quite capable of replicating the full ability of the internal mechanisms of the brain, however, with active guidance and intervention, patients can get very close. Secondly, it's possible that music training may act as a preventative measure for conditions involving the basal ganglia like Parkinson's due to how closely related rhythm perception and movement regulation are. The facilitated sequential movements associated with music practice and performance may be capable of mitigating the decrease in dopamine stimulation in the important motor areas. While this would require further research, identifying potential preventative measures for serious neurodegenerative diseases is incredibly promising. The final finding was that because music can affect and modulate the areas in the brain like the basal ganglia that are responsible for emotional, cognitive, and movement regulation, "effective rehabilitation of motor functions in PD might be obtained by acting on the underlying neuronal synchronization mechanisms through music therapy" (Maggioni et al., 2021). This largely reinforces the above findings, but it extends that various music therapy approaches are still effective in treating those with Parkinson's and that it isn't limited to aiding just one area of movement. In fact, in regards to the use of musical rhythm on improving movement and locomotion, "there is a general agreement about the promising value of music therapy in [Parkinson's disease]" (De Bartolo et al., 2020) across researchers.

The frequent and often adverse side-effects of many pharmacological methods of treatment drives a need for alternative or complementary methods of treatment that can be tailored to an individual's needs while simultaneously avoiding the unwanted side effects of medications. For Parkinson's disease, some of the most common side effects include nausea, low blood pressure, confusion, and behavioural changes like uncontrollable urges to engage in higher risk behaviour like gambling and sex.

There is significant literature in those with Parkinson's disease and one study by De Bartolo et al. (2020) aimed to further identify ways that music might improve gait performance. Gait refers to somebody's limb movement during locomotion, such as walking or running, and could also be described as somebody's stride. A gait disorder or a change in one's usual gait cycle can be caused by degenerative diseases like arthritis, neurological disease, or damage such as with Parkinson's disease or injury. While testing the effect of various

Brenden Hiebert

kinds of music on gait performance, they found that classical tracks including pieces by Chopin and Beethoven "had the effect of slowing the walking speed of all the three groups." Furthermore, the range of tilt in anteroposterior motion was also reduced while the overall duration of each stride increased. This may be due to the average tempo of the pieces that were played based on what we know about musical cues and Parkinson's disease. Interestingly, the range of oblique motion changed depending on the type of music with some increasing and others decreasing. This kind of result suggests that there should be more research into how music could be helpful in stimulating motion and also "counteracting the muscle rigidity that is another clinical feature usually associated with Parkinson's disease" (De Bartolo et al., 2020). Due to the nature of the results, it is possible that music therapy in this context could generalize to other neurological diseases such as Multiple Sclerosis in aiding movement and caring to the emotional well-being of those patients. Studies like the ones discussed further explore the need for standardized application of music therapy in various medical contexts.

Chapter 8 References:
De Bartolo, D., Morone, G., Giordani, G., Antonucci, G., Russo, V., Fusco, A., Marinozzi, F.,
Bini, F., Spitoni, G. F., Paolucci, S., & Iosa, M. (2020). Effect of different music genres
on gait patterns in Parkinson's disease. Neurological Sciences: Official Journal of the
Italian Neurological Society and of the Italian Society of Clinical Neurophysiology,
41(3), 575–582. https://doi.org/10.1007/s10072-019-04127-4
Maggioni, E., Arienti, F., Minella, S., Mameli, F., Borellini, L., Nigro, M., Cogiamanian, F.,
Bianchi, A. M., Cerutti, S., Barbieri, S., Brambilla, P., & Ardolino, G. (2021). Effective
Connectivity During Rest and Music Listening: An EEG Study on Parkinson's Disease.
Frontiers in Aging Neuroscience, 13. https://doi.org/10.3389/fnagi.2021.657221
Thompson, W. F. (2014). Music, Thought, and Feeling: Understanding the Psychology of Music
(2nd ed.). Oxford University Press.
Williams, E. T. (2019). Development of Regulative Music Therapy guidelines for early to
mid-stage Parkinson's disease. Australian Journal of Music Therapy, 30, 53–66.

Chapter 9: Addiction

Addiction can take hold of anybody, especially in this world of overstimulation. However, the exact definition of what constitutes addiction can be harder to identify. This may be because we frequently exaggerate or casually suggest addiction in regards to things that we're interested in or to describe a phase that we're going through. The Centre for Addiction and Mental Health (n.d.) provides four main identifier's to whether a behaviour should be considered as addictive or not. The first is the presence of cravings to use or engage in that activity. An example of this may be the craving for coffee first thing in the morning. Secondly, there is usually a loss of control in regards to the degree or frequency of use. This is to say that 'once in a while' activities may begin transitioning into daily occurrences or the average level of engagement with this activity may increase. For example, instead of one cup of coffee, it might begin to look like two or three. Thirdly, there's a compulsion to do it, which exceeds cravings to the degree that it is now a seemingly unstoppable urge to engage in the behavior, perhaps even at times that one knows that they shouldn't. Lastly, and perhaps the most dangerous identifier, is that the person continues to use or engage in this behaviour despite there being consequences in doing so. These consequences can range anywhere from somebody's health or financial situation to social and self destructive patterns of effect. These consequences are often distressing and can lead to the perpetuation and continuation of a painful cycle that is often difficult to break out of. Age, genetics, environment, mental health, and our learned coping mechanisms can all affect the presence of addiction in our lives and it is often a combination of these things that leads to addictive behaviours and long term distress. Lastly, it may appear that there is a significant degree of subjectiveness to this definition, however, the important link is that if something feels like a problem, or a loved one begins to suspect that there might be a problem, it's likely worth addressing and investigating whether or not a behaviour is just a flash habit or potentially something deeper.

Every person is different in what they like and this extends to the things that we may potentially get addicted to as well. One person may have no problem using a substance intermittently with little to no negative impact on their well-being while another may find it difficult to maintain a healthy relationship with that same thing. It's also important to consider the risks and side effects of the behaviours and activities to accurately assess the possibility of addiction. For example, a large percentage of the world could accurately be described as addicted to caffeine based on the frequency and degree of use for most people.

It is one of the most available recreation drugs we have and yet despite the morning headaches and afternoon crashes, there is little concern over its place in society. This is likely because while it does have its side effects, overall, most people see coffee as an overall improvement to their life. The hours of added focus and productivity outweigh the side effects and due to its overwhelming availability, it can be rationalized that for the average working person, coffee is an improvement to one's well-being despite the fact that we can develop a dependency to it. The same might not be said for illicit drugs that can hijack the brain's reward system and if allowed to, can gradually inhibit normal functioning and take over a person's life.

When discussing addiction, it's common to distinguish between physical addiction and psychological addiction. The main difference is the reason for which a person engages in that activity or substance. For physical addiction, the driving force for using is to avoid adverse side effects or uncomfortable symptoms as a result of not using. This is often the case with drug addictions as most substances alter the brain and body's state in order to feel the effects. As it wears off the body has to compensate and acclimatize to being without the drug. If the addicting substance is a depressant, some of the withdrawal symptoms may include insomnia, agitation, or anxiety. In the case of stimulants, withdrawal could look like fatigue, decreased cognitive function, and mood swings. The ability to rebound from a physical dependency can vary depending on the drug used, dosage amounts, and the frequency of use. For psychological addiction, the main motivator for engaging in addictive behaviour is usually for emotional needs which can be tied to our experiences and also our personalities. Both physical and psychological addictions can be difficult to break and they often coexist as two sides of the same coin, even if they can require different approaches to break. After all, "There is no "one-size-fits-all" approach to addiction treatment" (Centre for Addiction and Mental Health, n.d.). Furthermore, in recovering from addiction, relapsing is a natural part of the process and a result of the abstinence violation effect. It's easy to fall into a destructive cycle of relapsing and falling back into heavy use because of the guilt and other negative emotions that come with re-engaging with an addictive behaviour. What is important is reflecting on the behaviour and being mindful of the experience and what emotions were triggered in order to plan the best path forward.

It's no secret that live music and substance use are almost synonymous with each other, especially when it comes to raves, rock shows, and festivals. Beyond this, many famous musicians have been known to use and write about drugs and alcohol in their music. The notorious 27 club refers to famous artists and celebrities passing away before their 28th birthday with drugs and alcohol frequently playing a role in mortality. For these reasons, it can be seen that music may play a role in perpetuating substance use as part of the culture and experience of certain kinds of music and shows. As discussed earlier, recreational drug use doesn't necessarily translate into addiction for all people, however, for those at risk or with a history of addiction, these scenes may lead to problematic environments and people that increase the chances of engaging in risky and addictive behaviour. However, that isn't to say that live music is toxic to somebody dealing with addiction or other mental health struggles. In fact, the social bonding and sensory experience of being at a concert, especially one of a favorite artist, can be incredibly beneficial to a person's mental health. For people going through recovery of any kind, hearing a song from an artist that has gone through a similar thing can make them feel heard, seen, and related to at a time that they may feel alone or isolated from the people they love.

Chapter 9 Reference:
Centre for Addiction and Mental Health. (n.d.). Addiction. camh. Retrieved June 12, 2022, from
https://www.camh.ca/en/health-info/mental-illness-and-addiction-index/addiction

Chapter 10: Intimacy

While there are various ways to label intimacy, the overall meaning and purpose of the word is to refer to closeness. This could be in an emotional sense through empathy, vulnerability, and verbal communication or in other ways like through spiritual means or physical touch. Expressions of intimacy are crucial to the maintenance of personal relationships, be it romantic or otherwise, and this universal language is behind many of the personal connections that we keep. It is no surprise then that intimacy, in one form or another, has inspired countless songs and bodies of work across the span of human existence. Intimacy matters to us and music stands as a way to express the intricacies and trials that come with navigating it. Music in this way provides important support to many of the various psychosocial factors that come from relationships with other people.

From complementing our emotional state, to setting a mood, there are a wide range of ways music and intimacy co-exist. In general, intimate music often has a degree of gentleness that mirrors the way we approach a delicate or vulnerable situation with another person. This could mean acoustic instruments, moderate to slow tempo's, but naturally there are any number of combinations that can fit this description. Vocal music in particular can be very effective in communicating a specific tone or feeling because of the presence of lyrics and our ability to pick up on subtle performance cues from the vocalist. This supported with minimal instrumentation and recording techniques that make the vocalist sound in front of your face can create and add to the intimacy being communicated in the performance.

According to Statistics Canada (2022), there was a record low rate of divorce in the year of 2020 since 1973. While this statistic should be taken with a grain of salt due to the global Covid-19 pandemic limiting access to divorce applications and services, there has still been a consistent decline in divorce since 1991. This is most likely linked to the increase of the average age that couples are choosing to get married. In fact, common-law unions are also more prevalent which further contributes to a decrease in divorce rates since termination of these relationships doesn't count towards the statistic. Because of these reasons, young adults in Canada have been divorcing less than they were before the mid 2000's but for those above 50 years of age, the number remains about the same. This information suggests that there was a significantly higher rate of premature marriage in earlier generations. Also, since the rate of divorce is higher on average in younger couples than older couples, the decrease of divorce in this demographic significantly lowers the rate overall. More people are also marrying for love than ever before which translates to partners being pickier and consequently engaging in relationships that better suit their needs. Lastly, divorce happens for reasons outside of just issues surrounding intimacy, such as with infidelity, financial hardship, or other change that happens across the span of the marriage. However, a lack of communication, respect, equality, and displays of physical touch can all be linked back to the level of intimacy shared between two people, displaying how important maintaining that is to a healthy marriage. Fortunately, recent statistics show that, "Almost one-third of divorces are now the result of a joint application by both spouses" (Statistics Canada, 2022). This suggests that at least a third of couples are coming to a consensus about their issues and reaching a mutual understanding at the end of their relationship. This isn't to say that divorce is ever easy even in the cases where there is mutual understanding, but it's a positive outlook for a scenario that frequently involves complex resolutions in regards to family, financial, and personal reasons.

Research involving music and intimacy is particularly diverse and explores a wide variety of topics that range from the impact of intimacy on art and creativity to the role that music plays in arousal and romantic stimulation. Thompson (2014, p. 212) states that the emotional states of two people tend to become more similar or homogenous when engaged in musical activities together which could suggest that music is an effective way to support conflict resolution or reduce the potential for conflict in general. However, there is room for further research on the extent that music can be used in couples therapy or in the dissection of intimate communication between partners. This lack of research may be explained by the fact that every relationship and person is different and that identifying common links across relationships in this way may not be entirely possible. The use of case studies could prove effective in identifying effective measures in specific relationships, however, there currently isn't a large enough sample size to draw broader conclusions from.

Chapter 10 References:

Statistics Canada. (2022, March 9). The Daily — A fifty-year look at divorces in Canada, 1970 to
2020. Retrieved June 14, 2022, from https://www150.statcan.gc.ca/n1/daily-quotidien/
220309/dq220309a-eng.htm
Thompson, W. F. (2014). Music, Thought, and Feeling: Understanding the Psychology of Music
(2nd ed.). Oxford University Press.

Chapter 11: Happiness

Our overall health and well-being is a major factor towards the quality of our mental state and ability to function effectively in our day to day existence. There is a need for us to maintain the multiple assets of our lives in order to have balance and happiness. One way that many of us navigate this is through music. From monotonous commutes to work, pushing a personal best in the gym, or getting over a breakup, we use music to complement our mood and emotional needs. It's effectiveness in this regard has led to extensive research and implementation of music by therapists, caretakers, and health practitioners in various clinical settings such as "hospitals, mental health and rehabilitation facilities, mental health clinics, drug and alcohol programs, nursing homes, correctional facilities, halfway houses, and schools" (Thompson, 2014, p. 211). While many studies show that the effects of music are temporary and do wear off following the cessation of the experience or treatment, not unlike other pharmaceutical solutions, there is strong evidence to suggest that long-term habits, including those involving music, frequently lead to changes in the brain and ultimately our behaviour. This is due to the brain's ability to adapt and reorganize connections based on experience, which is better known as neuroplasticity. It's feasible then to conclude that a lifetime of musical experiences used to reinforce our mental state would be an effective means of supporting treatment for ailments or other conditions as well as maintaining and improving our overall mental health.

Firstly, musical activities require significant amounts of attention. When playing an instrument, there is a high degree of concentration and thought process that goes into it. This overtake of focus can be effective at distracting or taking our minds away from uncomfortable or painful thoughts. This kind of expression can often be very emotional depending on the degree that the song matches or relates to personal situations. Furthermore, songwriting takes this a step further in helping us say things that we might otherwise have difficulty expressing. In fact, it's common that "people who have difficulty expressing their feelings in words sometimes feel more comfortable expressing these emotions through music" (Thompson, 2014, p. 213). Even the act of sharing existing songs that encapsulate a shared feeling can help with communicating and coping with a situation. In the case of just listening to music, it draws our attention not just because it's a strong sensory stimulus but because it is emotionally rewarding and can trigger the release of neurotransmitters like dopamine. While this may not take up our attention span to the same degree as actively participating in music, it can still distance us from troubling thoughts or feelings and put us in a state where we can better assess and process what we're experiencing.

Secondly, music makes us move. While this is frequently in the subtle ways of head nodding and foot tapping, dancing and other synchronized movements bring us pleasure and in the case of clubs and music venues, dancing can reinforce social bonds between those involved. This also requires a great deal of concentration and can bring on the sensation of living in the moment because of this. It's also physically demanding in a way that is fun, social, and in an environment that may seem less toxic than other fitness facilities or programs.

Thirdly, we each have a unique experience when listening to the same songs. Our own interpretations are influenced by our unique experiences and differences, but also because of the creative nature in which we interact with music. By nature, we build abstractions and meaning into music and we do the same when we process it. This is partly why we are able to consistently get the most out of relatable songs even when our moods and situations change. We are also tied to our taste in music and this can be a large factor in our sense of identity, particularly with teenagers who are at an age where they're starting to differentiate themselves from their peers. While these choices often set them apart from their siblings, or other groups, it also leads to a sense of inclusion elsewhere. Music in this way encourages connection and belonging between people and it can "help … fulfill a human need for contact, [and] promot[e] emotional health [while] avoiding the health risks associated with social isolation" (Thompson, 2014, p. 213).

Fourth, music frequently affects our behaviour in ways that we don't always notice. From commercials, to shopping malls, music is used against us all the time to define brands and ultimately convince us to spend time and money on products and in shops. It becomes part of the culture of a store that people can identify with. For example, while it may seem obvious that coffee shops and bookstores have very different playlists from clothing or toy stores, there is still notable differences between similar types of stores. Since clothing stores are so closely tied to identity and expression, they often vary a significant amount from each other in not only what music is playing but also in the volume that it's played at. The quality of our driving can also be affected by the type of music that we're listening to. Beyond being potentially distracting, especially if there are others in the car, louder music tends to increase the speed at which we drive. When considering that music can have such an immediate effect on our behaviour, even in ways we aren't always fully aware of, it makes sense that there may be broader applications of music into all sorts of areas, clinical or not.

Finally, while Thompson (2014, p. 214) explains that from a scientific perspective, it's difficult to pinpoint direct sources of well-being from music due to the way that the effects overlap with other factors, on a human level, it seems enough that it just makes us happy. There is still research being done to enable us to make deeper connections and draw stronger conclusions on how music interacts with various conditions, ailments, and human factors, but the beauty of music is in its versatility and universality. There isn't one thing about it that makes it so useful and "Like a Swiss army knife, the multifaceted nature of music means it can be used in many ways" (Thompson, 2014, p. 214). Whether it's for dealing with loss, supporting recovery, or just dancing in the kitchen, music has a place in making the world seem a few shades brighter.

Chapter 11 Reference:
Thompson, W. F. (2014). Music, Thought, and Feeling: Understanding the Psychology of Music
(2nd ed.). Oxford University Press.

Brenden Hiebert